TABLE OF CONTENTS

CHAPTER 1

INTRODUCTION

This thesis is a study to determine if cyberspace warfare is a candidate to become a new United States Department of Defense (DoD) core mission area. The research questions for this study are focused on two major themes. First, is there a threat from cyberspace that could adversely affect the United States in achieving its national security objectives? Second, is there a gap in the current U.S. DoD core mission areas that could address this threat from potential adversaries that use cyberspace as a means to attack U.S. vital interests? Finally, the methodology taken to conduct this study is to analyze, evaluate, and synthesize key U.S. strategic documents, cyberspace related books, journals, and other related materials to thoroughly investigate the need for a new U.S. DoD core mission area for cyberspace, defined as cyberspace warfare.

To achieve the national security strategy of the United States, there is a need to analyze if the new primary missions of the U.S. Armed Forces and the U.S. DoD core mission areas adequately address cyberspace warfare. According to Andrew F. Krepinevich cyberspace warfare is defined as:

> The actions by nation-states and non-state actors to penetrate computers or networks for the purpose of inserting, corrupting, or falsifying data; disrupting or damaging a computer or network device; and inflicting damage or disruption to computer control systems.[1]

To keep this paper at the strategic and operational level this thesis will focus on state and non-state actors conducting cyberspace operations in, through, and from cyberspace as a

---

[1] Andrew F. Krepinevich, "Cyber Warfare: A Nuclear Option," *Center for Strategic and Budgetary Assessments*, 2012: 84.

means to achieve their desired strategic end states. Through this analysis, a case is made for a new U.S. DoD core mission area for cyberspace warfare. The justification for this analysis is to address cyberspace threats to U.S. military strength and economic prosperity that could adversely affect the United States in achieving its national security objectives.

In the latest strategic guidance, "Sustaining U.S. Global Leadership: Priorities for the 21st Century Defense," ten areas are defined as primary missions of the U.S. Armed Forces. The last "Quadrennial Roles and Missions Review Report," define six core mission areas for the DoD to achieve U.S. strategic objectives. The new primary and current core mission areas do not adequately address cyberspace warfare as a way to shape the National Security Strategy (NSS) of the United States. However, they subsume cyberspace capabilities as a service enabler across all the mission areas. This approach does not address the art of the possible, but limits the U.S. in its ability to develop a strategic approach using cyberspace capabilities as a means to achieve strategic objectives. A proposed definition within Joint Publication 1.02 for cyberspace capability is: "A device, computer program, or technique, including any combination of software, firmware, or hardware, designed to create an effect in cyberspace."[2] Cyberspace warfare that uses cyberspace capabilities to conduct cyberspace operations could ensure the U.S. achieves its national security objectives.

Cyberspace warfare is a possible "game changer"[3] which will force the United States to assess and evaluate how it conducts operations in, through, and from

---

[2] U.S. Joint Chiefs of Staff, *Department of Defense Dictionary of Military and Associated Terms,* Joint Publication 1.02 (Washington, DC: Joint Chiefs of Staff, February 13, 2013), 71.

[3] Merriam-Webster, "An Encyclopedia Britannica Company," http://www.merriam-webster.com/dictionary/game%20changer (accessed March 27, 2013).

cyberspace. Cyberspace warfare could expose one of the United States' greatest strengths as a potential Achilles heel as pointed out in the latest National Security Strategy:

> The very technologies that empower us to lead and create also empower those who would disrupt and destroy. They enable our military superiority, but our unclassified government networks are constantly probed by intruders. Our daily lives and public safety depend on power and electric grids, but potential adversaries could use cyber vulnerabilities to disrupt them on a massive scale. The Internet and e-commerce are keys to our economic competitiveness, but cyber criminals have cost companies and consumers hundreds of millions of dollars and valuable intellectual property.[4]

It is evident that technology enables military capabilities and is a critical strength of United States military power. Leadership, training, and education are potential strengths of any nation or non-nation state actor. This paper does not specifically focus on those characteristics but assumes them as part of the entire system. Hence, taking away any strength levels the playing field with any potential adversary.

Cyberspace warfare is a reality and the United States must move forward to address this evolution of warfare. If cyberspace is used as a means to attack the United States, then it is relevant to investigate whether the primary missions of the U.S. Armed Forces and the DoD core mission areas adequately address this new evolution in warfare. A new U.S. DoD core mission area defined as cyberspace warfare could ensure that the United States maintains a distinct military advantage over all potential adversaries. Cyberspace warfare as a DoD mission area can meet the challenges of the 21st Century by incorporating cyberspace warfare into a strategic approach that can achieve U.S. national security objectives.

---

[4] U.S. President, *National Security Strategy* (Washington, DC: Government Printing Office, May 2010), 27.

To build the case for cyberspace warfare as a new U.S. DoD core mission area, this paper develops the argument by analyzing key areas that directly or indirectly support this evolution in warfare. President Obama's Executive Order on cybersecurity further reinforces a need to analyze DoD's role in cyberspace.

> Having run out of patience for Congress to act on a cybersecurity bill, President Obama has decided to take matters into his own hands. Obama signed an executive order on Tuesday addressing the country's most basic cybersecurity needs and highlighted the effort in his State of the Union address. "We cannot look back years from now and wonder why we did nothing in the face of real threats to our security and our economy," Obama said.[5]

This paper broadens the scope by analyzing cyberspace warfare as part of a strategic approach to shape U.S. National Security Strategy. Each chapter will focus on a particular cyberspace area that mutually supports another part of the whole, building a case for a new U.S. DoD core mission area. This paper is not a discussion on the authorities to conduct cyberspace warfare nor is it a discussion about the evolution of cyberspace capabilities to conduct cyberspace operations in, through, and from cyberspace.

In Chapter Two, cyberspace as a new domain is analyzed from the current U.S. DoD definition and is further refined to provide a foundation for where cyberspace operations are conducted. By understanding what cyberspace is and the fact that the United States has benefited from cyberspace will establish a foundation to analyze if cyberspace warfare is a candidate for a new U.S. DoD core mission area.

---

[5] David Goldman, "President Obama Cracks Whip on Cybercrime," *CNN,* February 12, 2013, under "CNN Security Clearance," http://security.blogs.cnn.com/2013/02/12/president-obama-cracks-whip-on-cybercrime/ (accessed March 23, 2013).

In Chapter Three, possible threats, operating in, through, and from cyberspace are analyzed with an emphasis on intent and the potential impacts to U.S. national security objectives. In order to understand why cyberspace warfare is a potential threat to U.S. national security objectives, the concept of cyber power is introduced. According to Joseph S. Nye, Jr., power is defined as follows:

> Power is the ability to influence the behavior of others to get the outcomes one wants. But there are several ways to affect the behavior of others. You can coerce them with threats; you can induce them with payments; or you can attract and co-opt them to want what you want.[6]

One definition of cyber power is: "the ability to use cyberspace to create advantages and influence events in all the operational environments and across the instruments of power."[7] The possibility of an adversary using cyber power as a means to enable its own concept of warfare could challenge the United States in achieving its national security objectives.

In Chapter Four, the nature of war and the evolution of warfare are explored with particular interest as they tie to cyberspace. The key emphasis of this chapter is on the consequences of failing to adapt to a new evolution of warfare that could potentially impact the survival of any nation. Defending networks, operating effectively in cyberspace, and having resiliency are three steps in the right direction but they fall short and clearly do not prepare us for an adversary such as China that employs unrestricted warfare with no bounds.

> Warfare which transcends all boundaries and limits, in short: unrestricted warfare. If this name becomes established, this kind of war means that all means will be in

---

[6] Joseph S. Nye Jr., *Soft Power: The Means to Succeed in World Politics* (New York: PublicAffairs, 2004), 2.

[7] Stuart H. Starr and Larry K. Wentz, *Cyberpower and National Security,* ed. Franklin D. Kramer, (Dulles, VA: Potomac Books, Inc., 2009), 38.

readiness that information will be omnipresent, and the battlefield will be everywhere. It means that all weapons and technology can be superimposed at will, it means that all the boundaries lying between the two worlds of war and non-war, of military and non-military, will be totally destroyed, and it also means that many of the current principles of combat will be modified, and even that the rules of war may need to be rewritten.[8]

However, if the United States adapts to this evolution in warfare, then cyberspace warfare could meet the challenges of any adversary that plans to use cyberspace as a means to achieve its strategic goals.

In Chapter Five, strategy is analyzed to determine how to develop an approach to achieve national security objectives. The interpretation of what strategy is and how it applies to cyberspace will provide context to developing a strategic approach using cyberspace warfare to achieve desired strategic end states.

In Chapter Six, the primary missions for the U.S. Armed Forces and the U.S. DoD core mission areas are analyzed from a cyberspace mission enabling or mission ensuring perspective. The guidance within, "Sustaining U.S. Global Leadership: Priorities for 21st Century Defense," focuses on key military missions for the Armed Forces.

> This strategic guidance document describes the projected security environment and the key military missions for which the Department of Defense will prepare. To protect U.S. national interests and achieve objectives of the 2010 National Security Strategy in this environment, the Joint Force will need to recalibrate its capabilities and make selective additional investments to succeed in the following missions...[9]

The ten primary missions are counter terrorism and irregular warfare; deter and defeat aggression; project power despite anti-access/area denial challenges; counter weapons of mass destruction; operate effectively in cyberspace and space; maintain a safe, and

---

[8] Qiao Liang and Wang Xiangsui, *Unrestricted Warfare* (Bejing: PLA Literature and Arts Publishing House, February 1999), 12.

[9] U.S. President, *Sustaining U.S. Global Leadership: Priorities for 21st Century Defense* (Washington, DC: Government Printing Office, January 2012), 1-4.

effective nuclear deterrent; defend the homeland and provide support to civil authorities; provide a stabilizing presence; conduct stability and counterinsurgency operations; and conduct humanitarian, disaster relief, and other operations. A core mission area within the Quadrennial Roles and Missions Review Report (QRMRR) is defined as:

> Core Mission Areas are broad Department of Defense military activities required to achieve strategic objectives of the National Defense Strategy and National Military Strategy. A Core Mission Area is a mission for which the Department is uniquely responsible, provides the preponderance of U.S. Government capabilities, or is the U.S. Government lead for achieving end states defined in national strategy documents.[10]

The six DoD core mission areas are homeland defense/civil support; deterrence; major combat operations; irregular warfare; military support to stabilization security, transition, and reconstruction; and military contribution to cooperative security. The analysis of the primary missions of the U.S. Armed Forces and the DoD mission areas will demonstrate that there is a gap in the United States National Security Strategy by not accounting for cyberspace warfare as a way to achieve strategic objectives.

In Chapter Seven, a scenario on the art of the possible combining all instruments of national power, affecting all war fighting domains, is presented to reinforce the need for a DoD core mission area for cyberspace warfare. This scenario also supports the idea presented by Andrew F. Krepinevich, "The choice is ours. Time is growing short. The best chance of addressing these dangers---or, better yet, deflecting them---is to start preparing for them now."[11]

---

[10] U.S. Secretary of Defense, *Quadrennial Roles and Missions Review Report* (Washington, DC: Government Printing Office, January 2009), 3.

[11] Andrew F. Krepinevich, *7 Deadly Scenarios* (New York: Bantam Books Trade Paperback, 2010), 353.

The last chapter will provide some recommendations on a way forward to ensure that the United States maintains a distinct military advantage over all potential adversaries in, through, and from cyberspace. The recommendation for a new U.S. DoD core mission area, defined as cyberspace warfare will ensure that the U.S. can defeat any adversary that uses cyberspace to attack U.S. national security interests.

The threats are real. It is not a matter of if but a matter of when a nation or non-nation state develops a new type of warfare to exploit an Achilles heel of the United States in order to achieve its own strategic objectives. The nature of war does not change, but warfare does, and those who adapt survive, and those who fail suffer the consequences. As new strategic approaches are developed to meet national security objectives, cyberspace warfare could achieve these objectives for the United States.

CHAPTER 2

BACKGROUND

This chapter explores what cyberspace is and how the United States has become accustomed to operating in and through cyberspace. This will lay the ground work for why the United States needs cyberspace warfare as a new DoD core mission area.

The creation and the expansion of cyberspace are relatively new. Cyberspace is an explosive phenomenon. "The internet has experienced a breathtaking expansion over the past two decades, from a small network limited primarily to the scientific community to a global network that counts more than two billion users."[1]

"What drove the requirement to create cyberspace was a response to the launch of the first artificial satellite, Sputnik 1, in 1957 by the Union of Soviet Socialist Republics. In 1958, the United States established the Advanced Research Projects Agency (ARPA). The following year, ARPA was designated by the U.S. Department of Defense as the lead in science and technology applicable to the military, hence DARPA. DARPA's involvement in the creation of the Internet began with an idea to link time-sharing computers into a national system. In 1969 the ARPANET was commissioned by DoD for research into networking and four nodes were created (Node 1: UCLA, Node 2: Stanford Research Institute, Node 3: University of California Santa Barbara, Node 4:

---

[1] Andrew F. Krepinevich, "Cyber Warfare: A Nuclear Option," *Center for Strategic and Budgetary Assessments*, 2012: 1.

University of Utah). Information was transmitted between each node establishing a

virtual collaborative environment."[2] Cyberspace was born.

Almost 53 years later, the U.S. DoD defined cyberspace as an operational domain.

"DoD will treat cyberspace as an operational domain to organize, train, and equip so that

DoD can take full advantage of cyberspace's potential."[3] The U.S. Joint Publication 3.0

defines cyberspace as:

> Cyberspace is a global domain within the information environment. It
> consists of the interdependent network of information technology
> infrastructures, including the Internet, telecommunications networks,
> computer systems, and embedded processors and controllers.[4]

A way to interpret this definition is to describe cyberspace as a man-made domain which

is made up of interconnected systems in a closed or open environment. Those systems

consist of hardware, software, and people. The hardware consists of any device that uses

embedded processors, enabled by software such as firmware, an operating system, and

applications in order to perform a function. The software consists of code that could be

of many languages, such as machine, assembly, pseudo, object oriented, or artificial

intelligence. The code interacts with computer hardware to enable it to perform a desired

function. The people consist of those who interact within this domain, such as users,

programmers, system administrators, wide area network managers, local area network

managers, hackers, and security specialists. For the purpose of this paper, a hacker is

anyone who manipulates code through nefarious means to gain access to a system in

---

[2] Defense Advance Research Projects Agency, "Creating and Preventing Strategic Surprise," DARPA, http://www.darpa.mil (accessed February 25, 2013).

[3] U.S. Secretary of Defense, *Department of Defense Strategy for Operating in Cyberspace* (Washington, DC: Government Printing Office, July 2011), 5.

[4] U.S. Joint Chiefs of Staff, *Joint Operations*, Joint Publication 3-0 (Washington, DC: Joint Chiefs of Staff, August 11, 2011), V-II.

order to achieve some desired end state. An example of this system of interconnected systems that introduces the witting and unwitting participants within cyberspace is analogous to the cyberspace gaming world. For example, a team of programmers designs a gaming environment that enables users to enter into this environment to accomplish some tasks with goals and rewards. The typical user (gamer) would enter this environment, with set parameters to do certain functions, which provides some form of entertainment. Some users would augment their abilities to perform certain functions by enhancing their gaming devices with scripts that would reduce their reaction time giving them an advantage over any opponent who is not using a script enabled device. Some users could boost their advantage by using software modules that manipulate the gaming environment to make themselves stronger and faster. Other users would use hacks that could interrupt the flow of data to another user, making them vulnerable to attack (degrading their connection, making them slow to react). Of course, this would present a problem to the programmers who designed the gaming environment. They would be forced to take measures to secure their gaming environment from these exploits by hiring security experts who could find, fix, and mitigate them. If not, the typical user who is just participating in this environment for some type of enjoyment will most likely leave, resulting in lost revenue and possible failure of the company. So what? Our financial and transportation systems are built on the same principles as a gaming environment. The same conditions could occur in each and every one of these systems having potential catastrophic consequences such as the cyber theft of billions of dollars or disruption of airline traffic that could result in a crash.

To reinforce this point, the United States and many other nations have become accustomed to the benefits of cyberspace as cyberspace expanded.

> With expansion came increasing applications for the Internet, which fed further expansion and still more applications, to include the rise of a cyber economy, financial transactions, widespread automated regulation of key control systems, an explosion in sharing and storing of information, the emergence of new forms of electronic communications such as email and social networking, among others.[5]

The typical users of these systems are trying to perform a function that enables them to enhance their productivity in one form or another. If skilled individuals can manipulate these systems with ill intent, the targeted systems could fail and cause potential catastrophic consequences affecting national security. To address potential risks to the U.S. critical infrastructure, the U.S. Deputy Secretary of Defense, Ashton B. Carter signed a memo, 19 Feb 2013, defining what a complex catastrophe is:

> Any natural or man-made incident, including cyberspace attack, power grid failure, and terrorism, which results in cascading failures of multiple, interdependent, critical, life-sustaining infrastructure sectors and causes extraordinary levels of mass causalities, damage, or disruption severely affecting the population, environment, economy, public health, national morale, response efforts, and/or government functions.[6]

This definition could drive the need and justify the requirement for a new DoD core mission area, which cyberspace warfare could fulfill. To appreciate the "so what," we need to explore the art of the possible as related to cyberspace and the threat. The next chapter will explore the art of the possible by examining potential threats as related to cyberspace and the impacts to U.S. national security.

---

[5] Krepinevich, "Cyber Warfare: A Nuclear Option," 1.

[6] U.S. Deputy Secretary of Defense, *Definition of the Term Complex Catastrophe* (Washington, DC: February 19, 2013), 1.

CHAPTER 3

THREAT

This chapter will explore what has already been demonstrated in cyberspace and provide an insight into the art of the possible when cyberspace capabilities are in the hands of nation or non-nation state actors with nefarious intent. The purpose of this chapter is not to identify any one nation or non-nation state actor as a threat to the United States, but to reinforce the demonstrated intent or capability that could potentially become a threat to achieving U.S. national security objectives. For instance, the Chinese People's Liberation Army (PLA) articulates the art of the possible:

> As we see it, a single man-made stock-market crash, a single computer virus invasion, or a single rumor or scandal that results in the fluctuation in the enemy country's exchange rates or exposes the leaders of the country on the Internet, all can be included in the ranks of new-concept weapons.[1]

To explore the art of the possible, it is relevant to have an understanding of the motives behind the hacker community and how it is categorized. Usually the purpose and intent of a cyberspace operation typically falls into the following categories: personal satisfaction, criminal intent, political purpose, act of terrorism, or military in nature. Finally, by examining some documented cases of cyberspace attacks and the potential ramification of the impacts on the people, society, and governments, will further reinforce the art of the possible and provide an insight into future warfare.

In 1999, the Chinese PLA published a concept for a new type of warfare called unrestricted warfare. Within this concept, the PLA laid out a strategic approach that

---

[1] Liang and Xiangsui, *Unrestricted Warfare*, 25.

integrates information and cyberspace capabilities to achieve their strategic end state for the 21st Century, to dominate the information environment by conducting unrestricted warfare against potential adversaries.

> Kinder weapons represent a derivative of the new concept of weapons, while information weapons are a prominent example of kinder weapons. Whether it involves electromagnetic energy weapons for hard destruction or soft-strikes by computer logic bombs, network viruses, or media weapons, all are focused on paralyzing and undermining, not personnel casualties.[2]

This blueprint for a new evolution in warfare, unrestricted warfare, is a clear threat to the United States and its allies. There are indications that the Chinese have used unrestricted warfare against the United States and its allies.

> China's extensive computer reconnaissance in the United States and other countries should cause other nation-states to take note. Cyber issues such as these should be seen in light of the ancient dictum that "a victorious army first wins and then seeks battle." It is possible that China's cyber strategy is already preparing to preempt U.S. systems if Beijing perceives a need to do so. More importantly, China's ability to hide the form of its attack will make it difficult to recognize a preemptive action as it unfolds.[3]

It is not apparent to most, but cyberspace reconnaissance is a threat to the United States. When analyzed, there are implications that cyberspace reconnaissance could set the conditions to exploit a discovered vulnerability. For instance, to attack the strength of an opponent you could find a weakness in a supporting system that enables the functions of the overall system. Air power has always been regarded as one of the U.S. military strengths as demonstrated during World War II, Korea, Vietnam, and the recent wars in Iraq and Afghanistan. If you attack this strength through an indirect means, such as degrading the onboard anti-jamming systems by injecting a cyberspace capability that made the system ineffective, it could change the outcome of a hostile engagement.

---

[2] Liang and Xiangsui, *Unrestricted Warfare*, 29.

[3] Starr and Wentz, *Cyberpower and National Security*, 475.

14

Another method is to conduct cyberspace espionage, to steal the plans for a system, then reverse engineer it, find the system's strengths and weaknesses, and develop a countermeasure to defeat the original system. The point is if the Chinese have conducted a cyberspace reconnaissance campaign against the United States, the conditions for success in a future engagement could already be set.

There are many reasons to conduct a cyberspace operation against a particular target. Hackers could act alone, in concert with others, organized as a group or organized as part of a nation or a non-nation state. The motives that drive a hacker or organized set of hackers, or skilled cyberspace individuals are many. We can categorize most of these activities based on purpose, intent, and motivation into one of the following categories: personal satisfaction, criminal intent, political purpose, act of terrorism, or military in nature.

Some, but not all, hackers hone their skills and demonstrate them to gain personal satisfaction knowing that they can do it. An individual, who hacks a computer system just to prove that he can do it, usually does it to demonstrate his abilities to himself or his peers. Just like any other passion, hackers thrive on recognition and reward.

> Hackers thrive on information in the same way that people thrive on sumptuous cuisine. What sort of information? Stuff like how to crack passwords that open the portals of computers, how to make a red box with which to make free telephone calls, how to masquerade as someone else when they send e-mail on the Internet, and how to boldly go where no one has gone before.[4]

This environment could create a pool of individuals with unique skills susceptible for recruitment into more nefarious areas of hacking that are criminal in nature.

---

[4] Michael Alexander, *The Underground Guide to Computer Security* (New York, NY: Addison-Wesley Publishing Company, 1996), 11.

Conducting cyberspace operations for monetary gains usually falls into the category of criminal intent. The thefts of services, software code, or currency are all motivations for the cyberspace criminal.

> The possibility of illicit profits, together with a low probability of detection or identification, can make cyber crime attractive. Criminal groups that lack the technical skills needed to manipulate computer code may hire the services of individuals or groups of hackers. Cyber criminals reportedly now sell or rent software products in online markets for customers to use to support their own cyber crimes.[5]

It takes resources to train an individual to master the art of being able to find a target in cyberspace, exploit that target, and manipulate the code on that target. This concept reinforces the idea that organizations need to recruit or train skilled hackers to achieve their goals. This also presents another challenge for the community at large. As these organizations and individuals become proficient in conducting cyberspace operations, their services and demonstrated capabilities could become entangled with other activities such as political activism or cyber-terrorism.

Political hackers coined as "hacktivists"[6] typically are trying to make a statement to further their cause. This is usually done by manipulating websites that are part of the government presenting a contrary view to the political group's position. Most recently the group Anonymous has demonstrated their resolve and hacker skills by hacking into the U.S. Federal Reserve. "And, now, someone has broken into the national bank, the Federal Reserve. A 21st Century thief breaking into files, not into metal safes. The mysterious group Anonymous has struck again, with a warning, this is just the

---

[5] Starr and Wentz, *Cyberpower and National Security,* 416.

[6] Jason Andress and Steve Winterfeld, *Cyber Warfare Techniques Tactics and Tools for Security Practioners* (Waltham, MA: Elseveir, 2011), 21.

beginning."[7] A trained and organized group with intent and passion for their cause clearly has demonstrated the possibilities of manipulating the information environment to promote their position.

Terrorist organizations have also incorporated cyberspace operations into their activities to further their cause. Cyberspace terrorism is not hacktivism but takes cyberspace operations to a level of violence by supporting attacks on designated targets. According to the U.S. Federal Bureau of Investigation: "Cyber-terrorism is the premeditated, politically motivated attack against information, computer systems, computer programs, and data which results in violence against noncombatant targets by sub-national groups or clandestine agents."[8] This concept of cyberspace terrorism is reinforced in "al-Qaeda's Twelfth Lesson in the espionage section which focuses on collecting information on potential targets such as government personnel, officers, and their dependents."[9] There is a vast array of information that when coalesced together provides the right amount of detail that in the right hands, potentially supports terrorists' attacks on government facilities, the public or elected officials. Cyberspace operations could enable terrorists in accomplishing their mission by collecting critical information on the intended targets. The threat is real, and the potential of a cyberspace enabled terrorist attack is even more dangerous as the art and science of conducting cyberspace warfare is perfected.

---

[7] Greg House, "Hacker Group, Anonymous, Hits Federal Reserve", *ABC New.com,* February 6, 2013, under "Under Attack," http://abcnews.go.com/WNT/video/hacker-group-anonymous-hits-federal-reserve-18424607 (accessed March 10, 2013).

[8] Dan Verton, "Black Ice: Cyber-Terrorism's Hidden Danger," In *Black Ice: The Invisible Threat of Cyber-Terrorism* (Emeryville, CA: McGraw-Hill/Osborne, 2003), 285-289.

[9] Dan Verton, *Black Ice: The Invisible Threat of Cyber-Terrorism* (Emeryville, CA: McGraw-Hill/Osborne, 2003), 119.

One of the most dangerous types of hacker is someone who is part of a military organization that is supported by a nation state actor. The ability to man, train, equip and organize for cyberspace warfare is a strength of any nation state that invests resources into such an endeavor. The "U.S. DoD Strategy for Operating in Cyberspace," states:

> The development and retention of an exceptional cyber workforce is central to DoD's strategic success in cyberspace and each of the strategic initiatives outlined in this strategy. DoD will assess its cyber workforce, requirements, and capabilities on a regular basis. The development of the cyber workforce is of paramount importance to DoD. The demand for new cyber personnel is high, commensurate with the severity of cyber threats.[10]

While the PLA states within their unrestricted warfare concept:

> … warfare no longer is an exclusive imperial garden where professional soldiers alone can mingle. The first challenger to have appeared, and the most famous, is the computer "hacker." This chap, who generally has not received any military training or been engaged in any military profession, can easily impair the security of an army or a nation in a major way by simply relying on his personal technical expertise.[11]

One could infer to meet this challenge is to develop a cyberspace warrior who is trained in the art and science of cyberspace warfare. The resulting potential cyberspace power that any nation could leverage would give that nation an advantage over those that fail to adapt to this evolution in warfare. Furthermore, the possibilities to manipulate the hacker communities from a nation state perspective could provide the necessary means to leverage capabilities that are limited.

> Solar Sunrise was a series of probes and attacks in 1998 that were initially believed to be Iraq intelligence breaking into DoD systems. This was a big wakeup call for the military. However it turned out to only be a couple of kids from California who were being taught how to break into systems by an Israeli hacker.[12]

---

[10] U.S. Secretary of Defense, *Department of Defense Strategy for Operating in Cyberspace,* 10-11.

[11] Liang and Xiangsui, *Unrestricted Warfare,* 45.

[12] Andress and Winterfeld, *Cyber Warfare Techniques Tactics and Tools for Security Practioners,* 13.

This operation demonstrates that non-state actors are recruiting susceptible hackers to conduct operations on their behalf. A nation state could employ cyberspace warriors, as part of its strategic approach to achieve its goals, especially if these warriors are resourced, trained and organized to conduct cyberspace warfare.

It is not "if" cyberspace warfare will happen but "when." Cyberspace operations conducted to achieve nation or non-nation state objectives is cyberspace warfare. Russia's invasion of Georgia in 2008 suggests that a cyberspace warfare campaign targeting key Georgian communication capabilities created enough chaos to set the conditions for a swift and decisive Russian victory.

Moonlight Maze demonstrated that a well-planned operation conducted through cyberspace by skilled hackers was able to extract sensitive information from the U.S. Government, related to nuclear and biochemical capabilities.

> Russia, like China, has been accused of conducting cyber activities against foreign states. The main U.S. accusation was a series of incidents between 1998 and 2000 that came be known as Moonlight Maze. These intrusions were reportedly traced back to a mainframe in Russia.[13]

This operation demonstrated how to conduct reconnaissance of a target, find the right target, and then extract the information for document exploitation. Document exploitation could provide the adversary enough information to set the conditions for the success of their operation.

Russia is also suspected of conducting cyberspace attacks against Estonia in 2007 to manipulate the political environment to gain a favorable resolution over a disputed war

---

[13] Starr and Wentz, *Cyberpower and National Security*, 475.

memorial. Some critics argue that this was Russia demonstrating a capability, as a proof of concept to set the conditions for a political or potentially military success.

> The attacks on Estonia might be viewed as roughly analogous to how the Spanish Civil War provided a testing ground for German, Italian, and Soviet equipment and war-fighting concepts…the Russians used the lessons learned from their experiences with Estonia to better integrate cyber operations with traditional military operations in Georgia.[14]

This leads us to the Russian invasion of Georgia. There is strong evidence that the Russians integrated cyberspace capabilities into their military operations to set the conditions for mission success. "Just as radio and radar were integrated into operations during World War II to enhance the effectiveness of military forces, cyber weapons appear to have been employed by the Russians to enhance their forces' effectiveness."[15] The main targets of these cyberspace operations appear to have been the Georgian's communication infrastructure, with the intent to cause chaos and erode the population's confidence in the Georgian Government's ability to handle the crisis.

Another cyberspace operation conducted against the United States, labeled as Titan Rain was suspected to originate from China. This operation was deemed a large scale cyberspace espionage attack targeting key U.S. Government agencies and defense contractors.

> In 2003, a series of computer attacks designed to copy sensitive data files was launched against Department of Defense (DOD) systems and companies belonging to DOD contractors. The cyber espionage attack apparently went undetected for many months. DOD suspected that this series of attacks, labeled Titan Rain, originated in China.[16]

---

[14] Krepinevich, "Cyber Warfare: A Nuclear Option," 24.

[15] Ibid., 25.

[16] Starr and Wentz, *Cyberpower and National Security,* 424.

One could infer from these cyberspace operations that the Russians and Chinese are testing new capabilities and concepts in an effort to level the playing field with the United States.

Stuxnet demonstrated a new level of sophistication that effectively achieved a strategic objective through cyberspace by targeting a specific vulnerability within a Supervisory Control and Data Acquisition (SCADA) system.

> Discovered in 2010, the Stuxnet computer virus that penetrated Iran's nuclear weapons program took control of key SCADA systems that directed centrifuges engaged in enriching uranium. Once in control, the virus directed the centrifuges to operate at unsafe speeds. This resulted in their physical damage, evidently in some cases to the point of destruction, requiring costly and time-consuming repairs, thereby delaying Iran's uranium enrichment efforts.[17]

The ramifications of the art of the possible are significant, because they demonstrate a way to kinetically achieve strategic results using cyberspace as the means to attack a critical national asset. This further reinforces the concept that cyberspace capabilities could be used in a national strategic approach using cyberspace warfare as a way to achieve national security objectives. If, in this case, there was a desire to delay the Iranian nuclear program by means other than traditional kinetic means, cyberspace warfare could be an option. Under Article 51 of the United Nations Charter, a nation has the right to "self-defence if an armed attack occurs against a Member of the United Nations."[18] Recently, the Iranians have accused Israel and the United States of this operation. In turn they have launched their own type of cyberspace warfare against the U.S. and Israel. "Two years after the Stuxnet computer worm attacked its nuclear

---

[17] Krepinevich, "Cyber Warfare: A Nuclear Option," 62.

[18] Charter Of The United Nations, "Chapter VII: Action With Respect To Threats To The Peace, Breaches Of The Peace, And Acts Of Aggression", United Nations, http://www.un.org/en/documents/charter/chapter7.shtml (accessed February 25, 2013).

program, Iran is increasingly turning to cyber warfare itself in a growing, stealthy confrontation with its enemies."[19] This is indicative of what is possible when nation states integrate cyberspace operations into their military to achieve national objectives.

It is clear that cyberspace is a new domain where individuals, groups, nation and non-nation states have engaged in some type of cyberspace warfare. As nations begin to adapt and develop new approaches to achieve their national security interests, cyberspace warfare is a likely candidate to meet the challenge. The threat is real, and there are national consequences if the United States fails to adapt to this evolution in warfare. The art of the possible has been demonstrated by such operations as the Russians using cyberspace warfare in their invasion of Georgia and unknown actors delaying the nuclear enrichment program of Iran. This leads to the next chapter in which the nature of war and the evolution of warfare are analyzed as they apply to cyberspace warfare.

---

[19] Peter Apps, "Cyberspace the New Frontier in Iran's War with Foes," *Reuters.com,* October 24, 2012, under "Tehran Using Cyberspace to Retaliate Against Westerns Sanctions," http://www.reuters.com/article/2012/10/24/iran-cyber-idUSL5E8LMIJO20121024 (accessed February 25, 2013).

CHAPTER 4

NATURE OF WAR AND THE EVOLUTION OF WARFARE

Throughout history warfare has evolved. Warfare changes because mankind continues to advance technologically, and integrates these new technologies into the art and science of conducting war. Cyberspace is a new evolution of warfare, conducted in, through, and from the cyberspace domain and having effects in all the other domains. Cyberspace capabilities and the actors developing, employing and adapting new tactics contribute to the development of this new type of warfare. Clausewitz lays out a case on war that argues "that the nature of war does not change, however, the evolution of warfare does."[1] Cyberspace warfare fits this very nature of a new evolution of warfare. This chapter builds upon the previous chapters to discuss the nature of war through the examination of historical examples that reinforce the idea that warfare evolves.

Those who adapt and incorporate new evolutions of warfare into their strategic approach gain a distinct advantage over those who fail to adapt. Cyberspace warfare is on the cusp of becoming an advantage for any nation that adapts to this evolution of warfare conducted in, through, and from cyberspace. However, if cyberspace technologies and capabilities are not incorporated into a strategic approach, there is a risk of creating a disadvantage that could threaten the very survival of a nation.

If the nature of war does not change then what are the constant themes? Carl Von Clausewitz states that: "war is not merely an act of policy but a true political instrument,

---

[1] Carl Von Clausewitz, *On War*, ed. Michael Eliot Howard and Peter Paret (New York, NY: Everyman's Library, 1993), 83-101.

a continuation of political intercourse, carried on with other means."[2] This implies that the military instrument of national power is utilized to achieve a desired end state that diplomacy failed to secure. According to Quincy Wright, "The influence of human nature on war may therefore be studied by considering the relation of war to: personal motives and personalities; of cultural attitudes; and of personality of ideas."[3] This implies that humans have motives that drive them to take or not take action during a crisis, which could lead to war. According to Baron De Jomini:

> …there can be no sound rules in war, the observance of which, the chances being equal, will lead to success. It is true that theories cannot teach men with mathematical precision, what they should do in every possible case, but it is also certain that they will always point out the errors to avoid.[4]

Although nothing is certain, the ability to reduce uncertainty is relevant as one applies experience to the situation at hand. This implies that experience is a key component to mastering the art of war, a factor that can reduce uncertainties in a complex environment. According to Clausewitz, "war is thus an act to force or compel our enemy to do our will."[5] Conversely, the enemy is also trying to force their will upon their adversary. Thus there is a contest of wills between friend and foe during times of war. One could conclude that the nature of war does not change but consists of four main elements: failure of politics, human dimension, contest of wills, and uncertainty. However, warfare has evolved over time, and thus changes. Cyberspace warfare is an example of a new type of warfare.

---

[2] Clausewitz, *On War,* 99.

[3] Quincy Wright, *A Study of War* (Chicago, IL: University of Chicago, 1983), 319.

[4] Antoine Henri Jomini, *The Art of War* (Radford, VA: Wilder Publications, 2008), 246-247.

[5] Clausewitz, *On War,* 83.

History has demonstrated that warfare evolves and those who adapted were successful while those who failed to adapt suffered the consequences of defeat. These historical examples reinforce the notion and potentially project that cyberspace warfare is a new evolution in warfare conducted in, through and from cyberspace having effects in all domains, which will provide an advantage to whoever embraces this concept. A brief analysis of this historical perspective is relevant to reinforce this point. Examples from ancient Greece, Prussia, and World War II are illustrated to present cases where innovative leaders adapted and modified their methods to conduct warfare and integrated them into their strategic approach to achieve their desired end states.

Alexander the Great conquered Persia in three years and then conquered Egypt and India in approximately nine years. This feat by no measure could have been accomplished without his insight and his ability to incorporate new technologies, tactics, and leadership into a new method to conduct warfare. He was able to maximize his operational art in such a manner as to achieve a decisive advantage over adversaries that significantly outnumbered his force. The core of Alexander's army was his phalanx.

> The phalanx was a heavy and compact line of battle which becomes a column on the march. The hardy and athletic Greeks often relied on a depth of eight ranks, though more were sometimes added for special purposes. The virtue of this formation is its solidarity, both moral and physical.[6]

To gain a decisive victory, Alexander abandoned traditional hoplite warfare and instead integrated Phalangites.

> The hoplite was the standard infantry of the time, while the Phalangites were professional soldiers, and were among the first troops ever to be drilled; thereby allowing the execution of complex maneuvers well beyond the reach of most other armies.[7]

---

[6] Lynn Montross, *War through the Ages* (New York, NY: Harper, 1960), 7.

[7] Ibid., 5-32.

He also incorporated light infantry and cavalry as a maneuver force designed to attack the flanks and rear of the opposing force. This combined arms warfare established Alexander's operational approach that gave his army a distinct advantage over his adversaries. The most significant changes which occurred to accomplish this style of warfare included the use of the sarissa instead of the standard hoplon. "The sarissa was 21 feet long as compared to a Greek pike, hoplon, by more than two-thirds."[8] Due to its greater length the Phalangites did not require heavy armor or a large shield which enhanced their maneuverability on the battlefield. The phalanx could move forward at a slow march attacking and pinning the enemy's center while the cavalry maneuvered to attack the flanks and rear. To prevent his forces from being split during maneuvers, he "built up a light mobile infantry force, consisting mostly of archers and javelin men, which became the new standard for the ancient world."[9] To ensure he had an accurate picture of his enemy's strengths and weaknesses Alexander utilized "lightly armored cavalry forces that would act as scouts and when engaged in battle they would arm themselves with a sarissa."[10] The culmination of these adaptations was not an evolution in the technology, but in the operational art of conducting warfare which evolved during that time period. This combined arms evolution in warfare (phalanx and cavalry) that employed a semi-static blocking force coupled with swift maneuver set the conditions for Alexander the Great to achieve his strategic objectives through decisive victories ensuring his conquests of Persia, Egypt and India.

---

[8] Montross, *War through the Ages,* 19.

[9] Ibid., 13.

[10] Ibid., 20.

From 1870 to 1918 the conduct of warfare in Western Europe was influenced by political, economic, social, and technological change. To gain an appreciation for the evolution of warfare during this time, we must delve into the conditions that shaped the events during this period. "The Confederate of Germany was established with Austria as the leading power as a result of the conclusion of the war with France in 1815. From 1815 to 1866 a desire to unite Germany as one nation was imbued among the masses."[11] Otto Von Bismarck, the Minster President of Prussia emerged as the leader to put this plan in action to unite Germany under one rule. Before Bismarck could execute his plan to achieve his desired end state to unite Germany as one nation, he had to establish the right conditions to ensure success. His plan was twofold, "one was to guarantee Prussia replaced Austria as the dominant power within Germany, and the other was to establish Germany as the dominant power in mainland Europe."[12] In order to succeed, Bismarck had to do a significant amount of political maneuvering to ensure that he could concentrate his forces to set the conditions for victory. From a social perspective, he had to instill a sense of nationalism within the German people, which was easily done as a result of the last century of war for it cemented the seeds of hatred necessary to unite the people under a common cause. From an economic perspective, Prussia had rapidly developed a cross continent-market which was empowered by the rapid expansion of the railroad network within Prussia that set the conditions for developing new technologies. From a technological perspective, using mass production, "Prussia produced large quantities of the Dreyes Needle gun and the Krup artillery piece which were both breech

---

[11] Montross, *War through the Ages,* 633-654.

[12] Ibid., 633-654.

loading, that enhanced range and fire power."[13] Finally, under the leadership of General

Roon, "Prussia developed a process to mobilize rapidly their army through mandatory

service and localized mobilization stations."[14]

The conditions were set for Bismarck to execute his plan to unite Germany. "The

Austria-Prussia war of 1866, which lasted 7 weeks, met his first goal to establish Prussia

as the dominant power within Germany."[15] By creating the conditions that made it

appear as if Austria violated a treaty and was mobilizing forces to invade Prussia,

Bismarck was able to unite his allies and the Confederate of Germany to mobilize forces

to out maneuver the Austrian forces. By the use of overwhelming firepower through "the

massing of artillery and the superior quality of the needle gun over the Austrian muzzle

loaded rifle, General Moltke was able to defeat the Austria forces at Königgrätz."[16]

Bismarck's second goal was met during the Franco-Prussia war of 1870, which lasted

seven months and ended with the defeat of France. Again, Bismarck was able to shape

the political environment to cause France to declare war on Germany by "manipulating a

message from Prussia to France which insulted the French, demonstrating the use of

information to shape the strategic environment."[17] This united Northern Germany and

Southern Germany as one nation. The deciding factor during this war was Germany's

ability to quickly mobilize forces faster than its adversaries, sustain it via their railroad

networks, and to mass artillery at the decisive point. The Prussians had adopted an

offensive strategy that rapidly encircled the enemy and then they massed their artillery to

---

[13] Montross, *War through the Ages*, 633-654.

[14] Ibid., 633-654.

[15] Ibid., 633-654.

[16] Ibid., 633-654.

[17] Ibid., 633-654.

defeat their adversary in detail. On the other hand, the French elected to adopt a

defensive strategy to defeat the Germans. As a result, the war ended with the defeat of

"France, the loss of the provinces: Alsace and Lorraine, and a war reparation fee of five

billion francs."[18] Through the integration of diplomatic, economic, information, and

military instruments of power, Bismarck had set the conditions for strategic success. By

adapting new technologies, modifying tactics, and developing the ability to deploy forces

rapidly, the Prussian armies gained a distinct advantage over their opponents who failed

to adapt. This evolution of offensive warfare that incorporated moving forces rapidly,

concentrated artillery, and the adaption of advanced firing rifles provided the means for

Bismarck to achieve his strategic objectives. Finally, Bismarck's grand strategy "to unite

Germany was fulfilled and established Germany as the dominant power in mainland

Europe"[19] and Bismarck became the first Chancellor of a united Germany.

The conditions were set for World War I. Hatreds were ripe as a result of

Germany's conquest of France and the unification of Germany as one nation. Without

delving into the details of approximately four years of war, it is clear that the lessons of

the Austria-Prussia and Franco-Prussia wars set the conditions for WWI. Again, France

took a defensive strategy while Germany took an offensive strategy. Germany

demonstrated again "their ability to mobilize forces quicker than their adversaries that set

the conditions for rapid advancement into France."[20] However, because of the lethality

of technology the war became mired into trench warfare. Although new weapon systems

---

[18] Montross, *War through the Ages*, 633-654.

[19] Ibid., 634.

[20] Ibid., 683-706.

such as the tank and airplane were introduced, it was too late. However, the lessons from WWI set the conditions for a new evolution of warfare.

At the outset of WWII, the Germans had developed a new strategy called Blitzkrieg Warfare. The main capability behind this new evolution of warfare was the Panzer and the Stuka.

> The Germans' mobility and striking power were combined by ten armored divisions and nine motorized infantry in the army of invasion. The Allies had as many tanks, but were employed in separate battalions for frontier defense instead of being concentrated, as in the Wehrmacht. It was in the air where the allies were the weakest. They had less than 2,000 aircraft to oppose 3,500 first rate Luftwaffe planes supporting the advance of their ground forces.[21]

In just two months, the Germans defeated the French and the British forces. Although the allies did adapt, the war lasted another five years at an estimated cost of 60,000,000 lives.

It is clear from the historical examples that warfare evolves, and those that incorporate new technologies, develop innovative tactics, and employ a new form of warfare gain the advantage over those that fail to adapt. Cyberspace warfare is a new evolution of warfare conducted in, through, and from cyberspace and having effects in all domains, as demonstrated in chapters two and three. The employment of cyberspace forces, supporting or supported by air, sea, land, and space forces to control vital areas of the cyberspace domain is a new evolution in warfare. Potential adversaries of the United States as stated previously are adopting new technologies and tactics to conduct warfare in, through, and from cyberspace to achieve their own national strategic objectives, so must the United States. The nature of war may be constant but the evolution of warfare changes. If any nation fails to adapt to a new evolution in warfare, it risks the

---

[21] Montross, *War through the Ages,* 806-808.

consequences of losing in future wars that could lead to the very demise of that nation. The next chapter builds upon this notion as it applies to developing a strategic approach to achieve national strategic objectives.

CHAPTER 5

STRATEGY

In the previous chapters, the art of the possible was explored. Without a strategy for cyberspace warfare, the art of the possible is potentially diminished. According to Baron De Jomini, "strategy is essential to warfare, and all strategy is controlled by invariable scientific principles, and these principles prescribe offensive action to mass forces against weaker enemy forces at some decisive point if strategy is to lead to victory."[1] Apply this to the cyberspace domain; to conduct effective cyberspace warfare against an adversary would require a strategic approach that provides the ends, ways, and means to achieve strategic objectives. According to Richard H. Yarger:

> Strategy is best understood as the art and science of developing and using the political, economic, socio-psychological, and military powers of the state in accordance with policy guidance to create effects that protect or advance the state's interests in the strategic environment.[2]

Therefore, this chapter will provide a way of looking at strategy and how to incorporate cyberspace warfare into a strategic approach to ensure national strategic objectives are achieved.

The United States has a strategy for cyberspace operations, but it does not address cyberspace warfare as a way to achieve strategic objectives. Within the "Department of Defense Strategy for Operating in Cyberspace," there are five strategic initiatives. The five strategic initiatives are:

---

[1] Jomini, *The Art of War*, 49-55.

[2] J. Boone Bartholomees, Jr., *The U.S. Army War College Guide to National Security Issues* (Carlisle, PA: Strategic Studies Institute, U.S. Army War College, 2010), 53.

Strategic Initiative 1: Treat cyberspace as an operational domain to organize, train, and equip so that DoD can take full advantage of cyberspace's potential.
Strategic Initiative 2: Employ new defense operating concepts to protect DoD networks and systems.
Strategic Initiative 3: Partner with other U.S. government departments and agencies and the private sector to enable a whole-of-government cybersecurity strategy.
Strategic Initiative 4: Build robust relationships with U.S. allies and international partners to strengthen collective cybersecurity.
Strategic Initiative 5: Leverage the nation's ingenuity through an exceptional cyber workforce and rapid technological innovation.[3]

The focus of this strategy is on building the cyberspace workforce; defending networks and systems; strengthening interagency cooperation; leveraging the private sector's expertise; working with international partners, and harnessing the innovations of the American people. This strategy addresses a few challenges such as developing a skilled cyberspace workforce and defending critical information, but it does not address using cyberspace as a means to shape U.S. National Security Strategy. The next evolution of this strategy must address conducting operations in, through, and from cyberspace in order to set conditions to achieve strategic objectives.

A possible way to develop a revised U.S. Strategy for Cyberspace is to identify the ends, ways, and means to achieve U.S. strategic objectives in, through, and from cyberspace. This strategy could be further refined by defining the acceptable risk. Acceptable risk is related to cost in resources, risk to national security, and identifying potential second and third order effects if implemented. A view from Yarger's studies is that strategy informs policy and policy provides guidance to develop a strategic approach with ends, ways, and means balanced with risk.[4] This method to develop a strategic

---

[3] U.S. Secretary of Defense, *Department of Defense Strategy for Operating in Cyberspace*, 5-10.

[4] Bartholomees, *The U.S. Army War College Guide to National Security Issues*, 53-64.

approach could be applied to cyberspace warfare to achieve U.S. national security objectives as stated in the NSS and NMS.

One of the most important steps in developing a strategic approach is to define the problem that is causing the crisis at hand. To define the problem, an understanding of the current situation is relevant. A method to analyze the strategic environment is to use the "Political, Military, Economic, Social, Information, and Infrastructure (PMESII),"[5] model to determine what factors are influencing the current environment. By applying critical thinking and reducing one's cognitive bias, a problem narrative could be derived. Once the problem is understood then possible options to address the problem using the national instruments of power are feasible. The next step is to develop a strategic approach. Finally to determine if the approach is valid, Yarger's method is relevant: "suitable as it applies to the ends, acceptable as it applies to the ways, and feasible as it applies to the means."[6] Once complete this method could assist in developing a new U.S. cyberspace strategy that will inform policy and achieve national security objectives in, through, and from cyberspace.

This method, to frame how to think about strategy, is reasonable to provide the art of the possible to reduce uncertainty in a very complex world. Strategy is the integrated application of the ends, ways, and means balanced with risk to reduce uncertainty in the strategic environment. The purpose is to achieve national objectives using all instruments of national power in cooperation or competition with other actors that are also pursuing their own objectives. This framework to develop a strategic approach can

---

[5] U.S. Joint Chiefs of Staff, *Joint Operation Planning,* Joint Publication 5-0 (Washington, DC: Joint Chiefs of Staff, August 11, 2011), III-8.

[6] Bartholomees, *The U.S. Army War College Guide to National Security Issues,* 53-64.

incorporate cyberspace warfare as a new U.S. DoD core mission area to achieve U.S.

national security objectives.

CHAPTER 6

MISSION AREAS

In the, "Quadrennial Defense Review Report (QDRR)," February 2010, "Operate Effectively in Cyberspace," is a new area of focus for DoD, but it is not defined as a DoD core mission area. The challenge as stated in the QDRR is:

> There is no exaggerating our dependence on DoD's information networks for command and control of our forces, the intelligence and logistics on which they depend, and the weapon technologies we develop and field. In the 21st century, modern Armed Forces simply cannot conduct high-tempo, effective operations without resilient, reliable information and communication networks and assured access to cyberspace.[1]

This reinforces the idea of a potential Achilles heel within the U.S. military instrument of power that relies upon computer enabled technology to conduct high-tempo combat operations. To address this potential weakness, the analysis of cyberspace warfare as a new U.S. DoD core mission area is relevant.

The strategic adjustment document, "Sustaining U.S. Global Leadership: Priorities for 21st Century Defense," January 2012, defines a primary mission of the U.S. Armed Forces to "Operate Effectively in Cyberspace and Space." This is not defined as a U.S. DoD core mission area. As defined, it limits the potential of how cyberspace warfare could become a U.S. DoD core mission area. Therefore, it is also relevant to analyze the new primary mission areas of the U.S. Armed Forces as defined within this strategic document to determine if cyberspace warfare is a candidate for a new DoD core mission Area. This would elevate "Operate Effectively in Cyberspace," from a primary

---

[1] U.S. Secretary of Defense, *Quadrennial Defense Review Report* (Washington DC: Government Printing Office, February 2010), 37.

mission of the U.S. Armed Forces to a U.S. DoD core mission area, defined as cyberspace warfare.

U.S. national interests are derived from documents such as the Constitution of the United States and the Declaration of Independence. These interests guide the formulation of U.S. National Security Strategy (NSS). The NSS provides guidance to develop the U.S. National Defense Strategy, which is published in the QDR. The QDR provides direction and guidance for the development of U.S. National Military Strategy which enables the Joint Force to fulfill its role in assuring national security objectives. The Quadrennial Roles and Missions Review Report (QRMR) states the following:

> Core Mission Areas and Core Competencies provide guidance to the Services and the U.S. Special Operations Command on the appropriate mix and scope of roles and functions to meet priorities of the National Defense Strategy and National Military Strategy.[2]

As of the 2009, QDRR and the 2010, QRMR there is no core mission area for conducting operations in cyberspace. Cyberspace capabilities are diluted across all of the current DoD core mission areas. They provide a service or enable mission success. This potentially degrades the ability to deter, defend, and defeat an adversary in, through, and from cyberspace. Why, because this fundamentally violates the joint principles of unity of command, economy of force, and mass as defined in U.S. Joint Publication 3-0. If the U.S. fails to adapt adequately to meet the challenges in cyberspace, then as history has demonstrates those who fail to adapt suffer the consequences.

There are six core mission areas for DoD as stated in the QDRR: "Homeland Defense and Civil Support, Deterrence Operations, Major Combat Operations, Irregular Warfare, Military Support to Stabilization Security, Transition and Reconstruction and

---

[2] U.S. Secretary of Defense, *Quadrennial Roles and Missions Review Report*, 3.

Military Contribution to Cooperative Security."[3] The use of cyberspace capabilities to conduct cyberspace operations as a new U.S. DoD core mission area could ensure success for each of these DoD core mission areas.

Homeland Defense and Civil Support. The main focuses of this mission area are "defense of the homeland and supporting the civilian authorities during times of crisis."[4] Cyberspace warfare could ensure the success of this mission area by conducting cyberspace operations to detect, deter, and defeat threats that use cyberspace as a means to threaten the United States.

Deterrence Operations. This mission area focuses on influencing adversary decision makers in order to set conditions favorable to the defense of the United States.[5] Cyberspace warfare could ensure this mission area success by conducting information operations in, through and from cyberspace, which could influence adversary decision makers to take actions favorable to the United States.

Major Combat Operations (MCOs). This mission area's purpose is "the conduct of synergistic, high-tempo actions in multiple operating domains, including cyberspace, to shatter the coherence of adversary plans and dispositions and render him unable or unwilling to oppose militarily the achievements of U.S. strategic objectives."[6] Cyberspace warfare is critical for the success of MCOs especially in a modern day conflict using high tech weapon systems. One example is the use of a cyberspace

---

[3] U.S. Secretary of Defense, *Quadrennial Roles and Missions Review Report*, 3.

[4] Ibid., 5.

[5] Ibid., 5.

[6] Ibid., 5.

operation to escort a high tech weapon system to counter an adversary's attack against this system.

Irregular Warfare. The main purpose of this mission area is to "win the support of the relevant population, promote friendly political authority, and erode adversary control, influence, and support."[7] The use of cyberspace warfare to conduct information operations, in, through, and from cyberspace could ensure this mission area success by detecting, deterring, and degrading the efforts of adversaries operating in the area of operation.

Military Support to Stabilization Security, Transition and Reconstruction. This mission area focus is on "providing assistance to severely stressed governments to avoid failure or recover from a devastating natural disaster, or assist an emerging host nation government in building a new domestic order following internal collapse or defeat in war."[8] The use of cyberspace warfare could prevent violent extremist organizations from interfering with a host nation recovery by detecting, finding, and mitigating risks to the overall operation.

Military Contribution to Cooperative Security. This mission area focuses on the following:

> Describes how Joint Force Commanders mobilize and sustain cooperation, working in partnership with domestic and foreign interested parties, to achieve common security goals that prevent the rise of security threats and promote constructive regional security environments.[9]

---

[7] U.S. Secretary of Defense, *Quadrennial Roles and Missions Review Report*, 5.

[8] Ibid., 5-6.

[9] Ibid., 6.

Cyberspace warfare could ensure this mission area's success by conducting cyberspace operations to detect, deter and mitigate risks that could destabilize a region such as violent extremist or transnational criminal activities.

Cyberspace warfare defined as a U.S. DoD core mission area could enhance the ability of the United States to counter threats to national security. As a U.S. DoD core mission area, cyberspace warfare would have a whole of government approach, as supported by the DoD's definition of a core mission area.

The latest strategic guidance has ten primary missions of the U.S. Armed Forces: counter terrorism and irregular warfare; deter and defeat aggression; project power despite anti-access/area denial challenges; counter weapons of mass destruction; operate effectively in cyberspace and space; maintain a safe, secure, and effective nuclear deterrent; defend the homeland and provide support to civil authorities, and provide a stabilizing presence. Each of these primary mission areas will require some type of cyberspace capability to enable mission but also ensure mission success.

<u>Counter Terrorism and Irregular Warfare</u>. This is clearly a critical mission area for DoD attested by over ten years of combat in Iraq and Afghanistan. Within this mission area, cyberspace warfare could ensure mission success. Terrorist networks are continuing to exploit our weaknesses in cyberspace to set conditions for their own mission success. "Al-Qaeda was using the Internet to do at least reconnaissance of American utilities and facilities. If you put all the unclassified information together, sometimes it adds up to something that ought to be classified."[10] Using cyberspace as a means to collect information on possible targets is in line with "Al-Qaeda's twelfth

---

[10] Verton, *Black Ice The Invisible Threat of Cyber-Terrorism,* 115-118.

lesson in the espionage section of the Al-Qaeda training manual."[11] Having the capability to detect, prevent and counter these actions is clearly something that could ensure mission success. The core goal is to "disrupt, dismantle, and defeat Al-Qaeda and prevent Afghanistan from ever being a haven for terrorists."[12] This will require the ability to find, fix, and destroy terrorist organizations, their financial supporters, and their training facilities. This will also require the ability to find and capture terrorist leaders and bring them to justice. Cyberspace warfare could ensure these types of missions especially if the terrorists rely upon cyberspace to enable their operations.

Deter and Defeat Aggression. This is another key mission area of DoD. "Our planning envisages forces that are able to fully deny a capable state's aggressive objectives in one region by conducting a combined arms campaign across all domains – land, air, maritime, space, and cyberspace."[13] This implies that DoD will engage and defeat adversaries in cyberspace, but also since cyberspace crosses all domains there is a requirement to ensure mission in all domains by integrating cyberspace warfare capabilities into all aspects of warfare regardless of where the adversary is posturing. Most weapon systems rely heavily on computer software and hardware to make them as effective as they are. This requires capabilities to ensure they are protected but also the ability to find, fix, and mitigate any risks to core combat capabilities which could degrade the ability to achieve this mission area objective.

> Today's infantry squad has communication gear, GPS, tracking devices, cameras, and night vision devices. The computer chip is ubiquitous and has become one of the U.S. centers of gravity. It is both our strength and could be turned into our

---

[11] Verton, *Black Ice The Invisible Threat of Cyber-Terrorism*, 119.

[12] U.S. President, *Sustaining U.S. Global Leadership: Priorities for 21st Century Defense*, 1.

[13] Ibid., 4.

weakness if taken away. The loss of GPS satellites would take away many of our advantages on the battlefield.[14]

This applies to all combat systems that rely on computer systems that optimize the efficiencies of their functions. In the hands of one of the best trained militaries in the world, these systems have demonstrated the ability to defeat any potential adversary. If you degrade, deny or destroy the embedded computer chips, or corrupt the software code that make these systems so effective then you take away a distinct military advantage. By taking away this advantage, an adversary could level the playing field which could set the conditions for their mission success.

Project Power Despite Anti-Access/Area Denial Challenges. A potential adversary poses challenges to our ability to project power; cyberspace warfare can provide a way to ensure mission success. To counter an adversary's ability to deny access to areas that are critical to U.S. vital national security interests will take innovative solutions such as found in aspects of cyberspace warfare to ensure mission success. "Sophisticated adversaries will use asymmetric capabilities, to include electronic and cyber warfare, ballistic and cruise missiles, advanced air defense, mining, and other methods, to complicate our operational calculus."[15] If an adversary uses cyberspace warfare as a way to deny access, then options other than deter and defeat are relevant. This could include the operations to defeat, conduct reconnaissance, counter-reconnaissance, and offensive cyberspace operations in order to achieve mission success. "A key effort is the ability to prevent and mitigate the impact of a cyber attack. Extend cyber domain awareness, establish an active defense, and provide responsible offensive

---

[14] Andress and Winterfeld, *Cyber Warfare Techniques, Tactics and Tools for Security Practioners,* 5.

[15] U.S. President, *Sustaining U.S. Global Leadership: Priorities for 21st Century Defense,* 4.

42

capabilities." [16] This reinforces the requirement for cyberspace warfare, which integrates defensive, reconnaissance, counter-reconnaissance, and offensive operations that ensure mission success in, through, and from cyberspace.

Counter Weapons of Mass Destruction (WMD). This is an enduring mission area for DoD since the end of WWII. The threat of WMD is further complicated by the introduction of cyberspace warfare and the potential ramifications of losing the capability to respond to an adversarial employment of WMD against the U.S., its allies and partners.

> There is little doubt that a major nuclear attack can meet the most demanding definitions of "catastrophic": triggering the utter overthrow or ruin of a state and its society. By contrast, a cyber attack against critical infrastructure is almost certain to be much less destructive than a large-scale nuclear strike. [17]

However, if cyberspace warfare is conducted against critical infrastructure and targets the ability to detect, deter and counter the employment of WMD then the potential catastrophic effects on a state could create the conditions of utter chaos leading to regime change and destruction of that state. The success of this mission area is paramount to the survival of the United States, and cyberspace warfare could provide an option to ensure it.

Operate Effectively in Cyberspace and Space. This mission area presumes that the capabilities developed and integrated into other mission areas are an enabler for successful operations in other domains. "Modern Armed Forces cannot conduct high-tempo, effective operations without reliable information and communication networks and assured access to cyberspace and space." [18] This falls short of the true potential of the

---

[16] U.S. Joint Chiefs of Staff, *Chairman's Strategic Direction to the Joint Force*, (Washington, DC: Joint Chiefs of Staff, February 6, 2012), 5.

[17] Krepinevich, "Cyber Warfare: A Nuclear Option," 76-77.

[18] U.S. President, *Sustaining U.S. Global Leadership: Priorities for 21st Century Defense*, 5.

ability to ensure mission success through cyberspace warfare. Clearly combat systems are optimized for maximum effectiveness with technology enabled by computer chips and software, and there is a need to protect the integrity of these systems. However, this mission area gives the impression that effectively operating in cyberspace is merely a defensive measure with emphasis on the ability to operate and to withstand cyberspace attacks through resiliency. This is very similar to a corporate information technology security model that puts an emphasis on information assurance. There is no doubt that this is needed, but it falls short of the requirement to adapt to an ever changing world as new evolutions of warfare emerge that could threaten U.S. national security interests. A new U.S. DoD core mission area defined as cyberspace warfare could fill this gap and ensure that DoD is prepared and ready for future conflicts that put the United States in direct competition with adversaries in cyberspace.

Maintain a Safe, Secure, and Effective Nuclear Deterrent. The ability to ensure that the U.S. nuclear arsenal is safe, secure, and effective is critical to national security interests. Cyberspace warfare could provide the ability to ensure that an adversary doesn't disrupt the ability to maintain a safe, secure and effective nuclear capability. Cyberspace warfare capabilities could be used to find, fix and mitigate threats to this mission area.

Defend the Homeland and Provide Support to Civil Authorities. Of great concern is the ability to defend the eighteen sectors of critical infrastructure that the United States relies on to ensure its way of life. Cyberspace warfare conducted against any or all of these sectors could have a negative or even catastrophic impact on the nation's ability to govern and secure its citizens.

By repeatedly disrupting critical infrastructure for short periods of time, cyber attacks could erode public confidence of the reliability of said infrastructure. The costs of such attacks would be paid in terms of some or all of the following: accepting substantial economic loss, adapting the infrastructure, or abandoning reliance on information systems to manage and support our critical infrastructure (returning to pre-internet, 1982).[19]

A cyberspace warfare core mission area could provide the nation a way to ensure that critical infrastructure is defended from any potential adversary that uses cyberspace to degrade, deny, disrupt or destroy infrastructure to set conditions to meet their own strategic objectives.

Provide a Stabilizing Presence. Sun Tzu states "that the greatest military leader is the one who wins without going to war."[20] An option is to conduct cyberspace warfare, using information operations as the means and cyberspace as the way, in which U.S. forces could reshape the information environment to counter any adversarial use of cyberspace.

Conduct Stability and Counterinsurgency Operations. One of the main goals of a counterinsurgency is to discredit the host nation's government by manipulating the information that the population receives. The Arab Spring phenomena demonstrated that the youth within the Middle East and North Africa are highly connected via social media such as Twitter and Facebook. Finding, fixing, and denying the adversary's access to these social networks through cyberspace warfare could set the conditions for successful stability and counterinsurgency operations.

Conduct Humanitarian, Disaster Relief, and Other Operations. A critical element for achieving success is to ensure that the communications from the host nation to the

---

[19] Krepinevich, "Cyber Warfare: A Nuclear Option," 54.

[20] Bin Sun, Samuel B. Griffith, and Hart Basil Henry Liddell, *Sun Tzu The Art of War,* (London: Oxford University Press, 1971), 54.

people is uninterrupted. Cyberspace warfare could prevent an adversary from using cyberspace as a means to disrupt a humanitarian or disaster relief operation.

To reinforce the justification for cyberspace warfare as a new U.S. DoD core mission area, it is relevant to analyze the alignment of the current core mission areas with a DoD organization that has the mission or the preponderance of capabilities to achieve end states defined in the NSS or the NMS. One could argue that irregular warfare is aligned with USSOCOM, homeland security and civil support is aligned with the Department of Homeland Security and USNORTHCOM, and major combat operations are aligned with the services and the geographic combatant commands. Although cyberspace warfare is not defined as a U.S. DoD core mission area, "Operate Effectively in Cyberspace and Space" is defined as a primary mission of the U.S. Armed Services. The following establishes the lead for cyberspace:

> At all levels, DoD will organize, train, and equip for the complex challenges and vast opportunities of cyberspace. To this end, the Secretary of Defense has assigned cyberspace mission responsibilities to United States Strategic Command (USSTRATCOM), the other Combatant Commands, and the Military Departments. Given its need to ensure the ability to operate effectively in cyberspace and efficiently organize its resources, DoD established U.S. Cyber Command (USCYBERCOM) as a sub-unified command of USSTRATCOM.[21]

If cyberspace warfare became a U.S. DoD core mission area then USCYBERCOM would logically become the lead U.S. DoD organization with the mission to conduct operations in, through, and from cyberspace to achieve the desired end states within the NSS and NMS.

Cyberspace warfare as a new U.S. DoD core mission area could meet the challenges of an ever adapting, innovative and challenging adversary operating in a

---

[21] U.S. Secretary of Defense, *Department of Defense Strategy for Operating in Cyberspace*, 5.

complex strategic environment where cyberspace becomes the battleground of future wars.

> Our national security is inextricably linked to the cyberspace domain, where conflict is not limited by geography or time. The expanding use of cyberspace places United States' interests at greater risk from cyber threats and vulnerabilities. Cyberspace actors can operate globally, within our own borders, and within the borders of our allies.[22]

It is clear that each U.S. DoD core mission area and each primary mission area of the U.S. Armed Forces require some cyberspace capabilities to enable mission success. It is also evident that by diluting cyberspace capabilities across all the mission areas limits the ability to conduct cyberspace warfare as part of a strategic approach that could ensure mission success. Instead of diluting cyberspace capabilities across the mission areas, it could be more advantageous if cyberspace capabilities were incorporated into a new U.S. DoD core mission area that concentrates capabilities to produce decisive results that maximize effects to achieve a desired end state. Reinforced by the analysis of the current DoD core mission areas, the primary mission of the U.S. Armed Forces, and the apparent alignment of mission areas with U.S. DoD organizations, cyberspace warfare is a mission for which the Department of Defense is uniquely responsible. Aligning cyberspace warfare with USCYBERCOM will consolidate the preponderance of U.S. Government capabilities. USCYBERCOM would then become the U.S. Government lead for achieving end states defined in national strategy documents as related to conducting operations in, through and from cyberspace. Defining cyberspace warfare as a DoD core mission area would elevate cyberspace warfare from mission enabling to mission ensuring and provide the United States an opportunity to gain an advantage in cyberspace

---

[22] U.S. Secetary of Defense, *Quadrennial Roles and Missions Review Report*, 14-15.

without risking the nation's security by failing to adapt to a change in warfare. The next chapter reinforces the requirement for a new DoD mission area by demonstrating the art of the possible with a scenario that focuses on cyberspace warfare against the United States and its allies.

CHAPTER 7

SCENARIO

This chapter offers a fictitious scenario of the art of the possible by leveraging concepts introduced within Krepinevich's book "7 Deadly Scenarios." This scenario is an example of a possible approach by a fictitious adversary of the United States and its allies to conduct cyberspace warfare to achieve strategic objectives.

The adversary of the United States is country ABC. The target of country ABC is a United States ally, country XYZ. The main effort of this operation involves the Cyberspace Warfare Division, of country ABC. The plan is broken into six phases in order to set the conditions for the overthrow of country XYZ.

Erode Trust in Government. Conduct cyberspace warfare that degrades the host nation's ability to respond to a crisis. Create conditions that demonstrate its ineffectiveness. Conduct cyberspace operations against government communication systems focusing on websites that disseminate information to the public. Change information on critical government sites to portray misinformation such as false evacuation routes. The purpose is to create conditions where the people distrust their government's ability to govern.

Attack Critical Infrastructure. Conduct cyberspace warfare that degrades, disrupts, or denies services that the host nation relies on for its economic prosperity and ability to sustain its way of life. The U.S. Department of Homeland Security states:

> Critical infrastructure are the assets, systems, and networks, whether physical or virtual, so vital to the United States that their incapacitation or destruction would

have a debilitating effect on security, national economic security, public health or safety, or any combination thereof.[1]

By attacking the host nation's critical infrastructure, cyberspace warfare could set the conditions to erode the people's confidence in their government and create chaos at the right time that can be exploited by other means in order to achieve strategic objectives.

Conduct Espionage. Conduct cyberspace warfare that undermines the host nation's reliance on advanced technological capabilities to gain a distinct military advantage over any adversary. Conduct operations through cyberspace that gain access to the defense industrial base of the host nation in order to steal their latest plans on any force modernization programs. Find any partners that are collaborating on plans, and exploit their systems in order to gain access to their data. Captured plans could then provide enough information to reduce costs to weapons development programs, identify weaknesses that could be exploited, and provide the means to make their weapon systems ineffective at the right time and place.

Divide and Conquer. Conduct cyberspace warfare to create friction between allies and partners in order to delay or prevent timely responses to an immediate crisis. Create tension between the host nation's population and government to break their will in supporting any possible war. The purpose is to find the pressure points to break the political will of the host nation and any of their allies creating the conditions of no response or a delayed response. This could create an opportunity to achieve strategic objectives by gaining time to set the conditions for success.

---

[1] U.S. Department of Homeland Security, "Critical Infrastructure Sectors," http://www.dhs.gov/critical-infrastructure-sectors (accessed February 25, 2013).

<u>Slow and Steady.</u> Conduct cyberspace warfare that creates conditions of plausible deniability. Exploit loopholes in the host nation's or allies' ability to gain attribution. Continue to maintain access on critical targets and execute at the right time and place in order to set conditions for mission success.

<u>Twist the Knife.</u> Conduct cyberspace warfare that is synchronized to achieve maximum effect on the intended targets creating total collapse of the host nation's ability to respond to the crisis at hand.

June 2013: Country ABC, their Cyberspace Warfare Division receives orders from higher authority. The mission is as follows: Immediately conduct cyberspace warfare against the United States and its allies, in order to set the conditions for the overthrow of the government of XYZ by subversion or force, to coincide with U.S. and country XYZ Presidential elections, November 2016. If elections in XYZ fail to elect a government favorable to our strategic goals, then a full scale invasion of XYZ is planned for November, 2016. Subversion: conduct cyberspace warfare against key government officials in the country of XYZ, the United States, and its allies. Destroy leadership character and expose their flaws. The purpose is to discredit elected officials that are opposed to our strategic interests within the region and to get new officials elected that are favorable to our goals. Cyberspace warfare against the United States, its allies, and country XYZ begins.

July 2013: Cyberspace Warfare Division elements receive their mission to conduct reconnaissance of potential targets in country XYZ, the United States and its allies.

U.S. Computer Emergency Response Team (CERT) reports increased activity on all network intrusion and prevention systems protecting U.S. Department of Defense networks.

August 2013: U.S. news agencies report unknown hackers have gained access to Department of State, Pentagon, U.S. Treasury and other U.S. Government networks.

September 2013: Reconnaissance and exploitation of country ABC provides a detailed recommended target list to the Cyberspace Warfare Division Chief. Target list includes government officials; senior military leaders; defense industrial base; key defense partners; critical infrastructure; government websites, and various other secondary targets of country ABC.

October 2013: U.S. news agency reports unknown hackers gain access to a major defense contractor working on advanced precision guided systems. Detail on what was taken is not known at this time.

November 2013: County XYZ news agency reports that websites containing the list of all government officials was compromised by unknown hackers.

December 2013: Canadian and British defense partners of the U.S. report unknown hackers had gained access to sensitive research and development programs linked to an anti-jamming system.

January 2014: U.S. Senator John Smith's relationship with a Florida woman was exposed, detailing a two year affair. Senator John Smith is up for re-election in 2014 and he is a strong supporter of the U.S. bilateral defense agreement with country XYZ.

February 2014: Country XYZ reports unknown hackers gained access to their weapons development program on a future anti-ballistic missile system, co-sponsored by the U.S.

March 2014: Pentagon issues a new directive that focuses on counter cyberspace espionage. U.S. public is outraged as details of this plan indicate increased monitoring of U.S. public communications. This could infringe upon the right of freedom of speech.

April 2014: The hacker organizations Anonymous post the Pentagon's new counter cyberspace espionage directive on major websites. Pentagon officials report that some of the information posted was incorrect or was modified. U.S. public is outraged and demands justice. Litigation is initiated by a group of concerned U.S. citizens to prevent this directive from being implemented.

May 2014: U.S. oil companies report unknown hackers gained unauthorized access to some of their offshore platforms.

June 2014: Country XYZ's news agencies report that President of XYZ is suspected of running a corrupt government and has been pocketing tax revenues to fund his extravagant life style. These reports have been unsubstantiated but were leaked from an unidentified source.

July 2014: Key government officials of country XYZ have been indicted on racketeering. Information was provided to the police by an anonymous email that contained various facts linking the officials to various crime organizations.

August 2014: Unconfirmed reports state that Anonymous gained access to the Pentagon email system.

September 2014: U.S. senior military officials are embarrassed and some resign over scandals that allude to inappropriate handling of funds, affairs and making statements opposing the administration's handling of the war in Afghanistan. Further investigations reveal that emails and various documents were released to multiple news agencies by an unknown person.

October 2014: Unknown hackers gained access to various political websites, Twitter, and Facebook accounts and manipulated key political officials' statements and positions on sensitive political issues.

November 2014: U.S. Senate and House majority are changed. Attitudes among the new elected officials lean towards domestic issues and on North and South America relations. Some members within Congress are already pushing for a new strategic shift to look inward and are requesting a review of all bilateral defense agreements.

December 2014: A major U.S. defense contractor reports that their systems were accessed by unknown hackers. On further investigations, key plans on future fighter systems were stolen.

January 2015: U.S. Congress repeals the U.S. Patriot Act. U.S. news agency reports embedded processors shipped to a U.S. Defense contractor were corrupted. Initial reports suspect the computer chips were infected somewhere along the defense supply chain.

February 2015: Government officials in the U.K. are upset over the speeches from the President from XYZ. President of XYZ condemns the U.K.'s recent military operations in the Middle East.

March 2015: U.S. experiences power outages in the Northwest lasting for upwards of 20 minutes.

April 2015: U.S Defense partners in Europe report their systems were accessed by unknown hackers, stealing plans on the new Joint Fighter.

May 2015: U.S. and XYZ conduct joint military exercises. Country ABC protests the exercises as it threatens the stability within the region. Information on the plans of the U.S.-XYZ exercise is leaked to the U.S. public. U.S. public responds with outrage, over a potential conflict in a region that they don't believe the U.S. has any interests.

June 2015: U.S attack helicopter crashes due to a software glitch in the avionics system. Preliminary investigations report some data was corrupted that might have caused the software glitch.

July 2015: U.S water and sewage systems experience outages in the state of Illinois. No evidence of foul play, but the investigation is ongoing.

August 2015: Country XYZ President's financial records are revealed on the internet posted to various websites across the country. Allegation of corruption surfaces among various news agencies within the country of XYZ. Members of Congress from various states push to break diplomatic ties with the corrupt government of XYZ.

September 2015: Country XYZ's critical infrastructure systems experience outages. Government of XYZ accuses country ABC of conducting cyberspace warfare against their critical infrastructure. Country ABC denies all allegations.

March 2016: The Pentagon accuses country ABC of conducting cyberspace warfare against the U.S. and country XYZ. Country ABC denies all allegations. Country ABC presents its case to the United Nations.

May 2016: Country ABC unveils a new fighter system which looks like the U.S. future fighter system, scheduled for production in late 2016.

June 2016: U.S. government public alert systems experience temporary degradation in services. U.S. accuses country ABC of hacking into their systems.

July 2016: Country ABC accuses the U.S. and country XYZ of conducting cyberspace warfare against them. The U.S. and country XYZ deny all allegations.

August 2016: U.S. news agencies report unknown hackers removed over two trillion dollars from electronic circulation. Identity of the hackers is currently unknown. Within days of this report, the U.S. Stock Exchange, DOW Jones drops 1,208 points. Other world markets suffer similar losses.

September 2016: The U.K. and Canada back out of the defense agreement with XYZ. U.S. Stock Exchange drops over 4,000 points during this month. U.S. news agencies report that the cause for the stock market's plummet is as a result of the loss of over two trillion dollars.

October 2016: All U.S. forces are put on alert. Country XYZ puts all their military forces on alert. U.S. agencies report unrest across the United States, with groups staging protests against possible war with country ABC. U.S. unemployment reaches an all-time high of 15%. U.S. stock market has lost over 6,000 points since August with no signs of recovering soon.

November 2016: U.S elects a new President who is apathetic towards country XYZ's government. Country XYZ President remains in power, despite allegation of fraud and corruption. U.S. oil rig in the Gulf of Mexico explodes, causing a massive oil spill.

December 2016: Key military systems within country XYZ are grounded because of software glitches. U.S. 7th Fleet's C2 systems go black, cause unknown. The U.S. military bases in the vicinity of country XYZ experience degradation in the host nation power and water support, which delays U.S. forces from deploying in response to the crisis in XYZ. A coordinated cyberspace warfare attack on critical infrastructure within the United States and XYZ has shut down key government services, creating chaos across the public and private sectors. Country ABC launches a massive invasion of country XYZ. The ability of the U.S. to respond with sufficient military power is delayed due to the crippling effects of a concentrated cyberspace warfare campaign directed against the United States, its allies and country XYZ.

Although this is a fictitious scenario, the art of the possible is demonstrated. According to Nassim Nicolas Taleb:

> I stick my neck out and make a claim, against many of our habits of thought, that our world is dominated by the extremes, the unknown, and the very improbable (improbable according our current knowledge) – and all the while we spend our time engaged in small talk, focusing on the known, and the repeated.[2]

If the United States declared cyberspace warfare as a DoD core mission area this scenario could be avoided by developing a strategic approach that employs cyberspace warfare as a new DoD core mission area to counter any adversary who uses cyberspace to achieve

---

[2] Nassim Taleb, *The Black Swan: The Impact of the Highly Improbable* (New York, NY: Random House Trade Paperbacks, 2010), xxxii.

its own strategic objectives. In addition, aligning cyberspace warfare with USCYBERCOM will provide a national effort to engage adversaries in, through, and from cyberspace in order to achieve U.S. national security objectives. To achieve this national focused effort it is also prudent to leverage the public and private sectors by establishing partners, fostering relations and by breaking down barriers. USCYBERCOM as the lead U.S. DoD organization for cyberspace warfare could achieve this in accordance with the Department of Defense Strategy for Operating in Cyberspace.

CHAPTER 8

RECOMMENDATIONS

Recommend the United States Department of Defense define cyberspace warfare as a new DoD core mission area. Cyberspace warfare as a DoD core mission area will enhance the United States ability to develop strategic approaches to achieve national strategic objectives in, through and from cyberspace and develop a new strategy for operating in cyberspace. Without a dedicated mission area for cyberspace warfare, there is the chance that an adversary will exploit one of the United States greatest strengths, which is the technology that enables the military instrument of national power. To complement this recommendation consider exploring cyber power as a new addition to the instruments of national power. Finally, this paper and a proposed joint working group would inform the next Quadrennial Defense Review Report to create cyberspace warfare as a new DoD core mission area and recommend exploring the concept of cyber power as a new instrument of national power and investigate the similarities to sea power.

Cyberspace is the new operational domain. Adversaries and future potential adversaries will use cyberspace to achieve their own strategic objectives. The art of the possible has been demonstrated and it is not a matter of when the U.S. will be attacked but a matter of how soon. Currently the United States has a clear technological military advantage over any potential adversary, but this gap is closing. The United States relies heavily on this advantage; therefore this strength could be the nation's Achilles heel, unless innovative ideas are explored and implemented. The idea to make cyberspace warfare a new U.S. DoD core mission area is critical. Cyberspace warfare could ensure U.S. national security interests are protected if it is incorporated into a new strategic approach that counters any adversary's use of cyberspace that threatens the United States. "The United States must create an effective national and international framework for the development and use of cyber as part of an overall national security strategy."[1] To accomplish this task, recommend introducing the concept of cyberspace warfare as a new DoD core mission area in QDR 2013.

This new strategic approach could then shape the U.S. strategic position globally by employing cyber power, as a part of the national instruments of power. According to the United States National Security Strategy "a balance of the Diplomatic, Informational, Military, and Economic powers (DIME) are essential to achieve National Security Objectives."[2] Reinforced throughout this paper, it is clear that cyberspace capabilities are essential to all the instruments of national power. Cyberspace capabilities enable the success of all operations supporting the instruments of national power. An option is to make cyber power a subset of informational power, which would align it with the definition of cyberspace as being a subset of the information environment. Another option is to make cyber power a new instrument of power, giving us DIME-C. The goal is to ensure that cyber power can meet the complex challenges that require a strong, agile, and capable cyber force whose actions are synchronized, coordinated, and integrated with all the other national instruments of power.

Another recommendation is to continue pursuing cyber power as a means to ensure economic prosperity similar to that of sea power. According to a recent article in the Joint Force Quarterly, "sea power and cyber power both primarily exist to protect

---

[1] Starr and Wentz, *Cyberpower and National Security,* 3.
[2] U.S. President, *National Security Strategy*, 1-52.

economic interests within their perspective domains."[3] As stated previously, power is

used to influence others to achieve some desired end state. Just as sea power has secured

economic prosperity for the United States, so could cyber power. The article further

states:

> Hard power will be secondary to soft power in cyberspace for the foreseeable
> future. Strategies aimed at attracting and co-opting will be more successful than
> those attempting to control through force. This limits the role the military will
> play in cyberspace, but it does not invalidate the need for tailored government
> programs and policies.[4]

The balance of soft and hard cyber power to achieve diplomatic, informational, military

or economic end states is similar to how sea power achieves like results. It is imperative

that we investigate the similarities between sea and cyber power and learn how to

effectively employ this new power in order to achieve national security objectives. It is

also relevant to broaden the scope and look at land, air, and space power as they relate to

cyber power.

Cyberspace warfare as a U.S. DoD core mission area can ensure that the United

States achieves its national security objectives. The preponderance of the cyberspace

capabilities would reside with the United States Government to man, train, and equip a

cyberspace force capable of defending the United States. The main focus of this new

DoD core mission area is to ensure the security of the United States in, through, and from

cyberspace against any adversary that uses cyberspace as a means to attack the United

States. It is also relevant to pursue if cyber power is either a new instrument of national

power or is a subset of the informational instrument of power. Another recommendation

---

[3] Kris E. Barcombs, "From Sea Power to Cyber Power, Learning from the Past to Craft a Strategy
for the Future," *Joint Force Quarterly*, Issue 69, 2d Quarter, 2013: 79.

[4] Ibid., 83.

is to pursue the similarities between cyber and sea power as it pertains to economic prosperity. These recommendations would require a joint working group to analyze and evaluate the need for this new U.S. DoD core mission area, cyber power as a new instrument of national power, and cyber power akin to sea power. Cyberspace warfare as a U.S. DoD core mission area, if approved, will leverage these concepts of cyber power as an instrument of national power to ensure economic prosperity is secured in, through, and from cyberspace.

CHAPTER 9

CONCLUSION

The United States needs a Department of Defense core mission area for cyberspace warfare. This new mission area sets the conditions to counter any adversary that uses cyberspace as a means to threaten U.S. national security interests. However, if the U.S. fails to adapt to this evolution of warfare conducted in cyberspace, it risks the chance of defeat with potential dire consequences.

In the current "U.S. Quadrennial Roles and Mission Review" and "Sustaining U.S Global Leadership: Priorities for the 21st Century Defense," cyberspace warfare is not addressed as a potential DoD core mission area. This shortfall fails to recognize the role of cyberspace warfare in shaping U.S. National Security Strategy. Operating effectively in cyberspace does not provide the scope and breadth to fully leverage the potentials of cyberspace warfare to achieve strategic objectives. As a U.S. DoD core mission area, cyberspace warfare as part of a national strategic approach could counter any potential adversary's use of cyberspace that threatens U.S. national security interests. This new core mission area will enable the United States to shape the strategic environment to achieve strategic objectives in, through, and from cyberspace.

The scenario in chapter seven reinforces the art of the possible, by conducting cyberspace warfare that attacks the human, social, physical, and informational dimensions of a nation, creating the conditions to achieve strategic success. By creating enough chaos, an adversary could set the conditions to attain its strategic objectives. Clearly, the United States has to adapt and approach cyberspace as a domain that can shape the national security strategy. Or else, we must wash this concept of cyberspace warfare aside as science fiction hogwash, and accept the risks of the possible.

The evolution of warfare has evolved over time, but the nature of war has not. Nations that have adapted to new technologies, incorporated them into their tactics and have nested them as part of their strategic approach have clearly been successful. Those who fail to adapt have suffered the consequence of their decisions. Strategy, warfare and war are all interwoven. Great leaders, such as Alexander the Great and Bismarck understand this. The United States has an opportunity to adapt now or become a nation that lost its innovative edge and failed to adapt.

There is no doubt that the United States relies upon cyberspace to enable its economic prosperity. Cyberspace capabilities that enable the world's most technologically advanced military also ensure a way of life that most Americans have become accustomed. This cyberspace enabled technology is one of many strengths of the United States, but it could also become its Achilles heel. All of the best weapons systems in the world do no good at the right time and place if those systems are corrupted, degraded, or just ineffective due to a cyberspace attack. To ensure that the U.S. way of life is maintained, and U.S. national security interests are protected, the United States must adapt to warfare conducted in cyberspace. Cyberspace warfare as a U.S. DoD core mission area will ensure that the United States achieves its national security objectives as stated within the NSS and NMS.

BIBLIOGRAPHY

Alberts, David S., John Garstka, and Frederick P. Stein. *Network Centric Warfare: The Face of Battle in the 21st Century*. Washington, DC: National Defense University Press, 1999.

Alexander, Michael. *The Underground Guide to Computer Security: Slightly Askew Advice on Protecting Your PC and What's On It*. Reading, MA: Addison-Wesley Pub., 1996.

Andress, Jason, Steve Winterfeld, and Russ Rogers. *Cyber Warfare: Techniques, Tactics and Tools for Security Practitioners*. Amsterdam: Syngress/Elsevier, 2011.

Apps, Peter. "Cyberspace the New Frontier in Iran's War With Foes." *Reuters.com*. October 24, 2012. http://www.reuters.com/article/2012/10/24/iran-cyber-idUSL5E8LMIJO20121024 (accessed February 25, 2013).

Bartholomees, J. Boone. *The U.S. Army War College Guide to National Security Issues*. Carlisle, PA: Strategic Studies Institute, U.S. Army War College, 2010.

Charter of the United Nations. "Chapter VII: Action With Respect to Threats to the Peace, Breaches of the Peace, and Acts of Aggression." United Nations. http://www.un.org/en/documents/charter/chapter7.shtml (accessed February 25, 2013).

Clarke, Richard A., and Robert K. Knake. *Cyber War: The Next Threat to National Security and What to Do About It*. New York: Ecco, 2010.

Clausewitz, Carl Von. *On War*. Ed. Michael Eliot Howard and Peter Paret. New York: Everyman's Library, 1993.

Corbett, Julian Stafford. *Principles of Maritime Strategy*. Mineola, NY: Dover Publications, 2004.

Defense Advanced Research Projects Agency. "Creating and Preventing Strategic Surprise." DARPA. http://www.darpa.mil (accessed February 25, 2013).

Engleman, Eric. "Obama Orders Cybersecurity Standards for Infrastructure." *Bloomberg.com*. February 13, 2013. http://www.bloomberg.com/news/2013-02-13/obama-orders-cybersecurity-standards-for-u-s-infrastructure.html (accessed February 20, 2013).

Fuller, J. F. C. *The Conduct of War, 1789-1961: A Study of the Impact of the French, Industrial, and Russian Revolutions on War and Its Conduct*. New York: Da Capo, 1992.

Hanson, Victor Davis. *The Western Way of War: Infantry Battle in Classical Greece*. Berkeley: University of California, 2000.

House, Greg. "Hacker Group, Anonymous, Hits Federal Reserve." *ABCnews.go.com.* February 6, 2013. http://abcnews.go.com/WNT/video/hacker-group-anonymous-hits-federal-reserve-18424607 (accessed March 10, 2013).

Jomini, Antoine Henri. *The Art of War*. Radford,VA: Wilder Publications, 2008.

Kramer, Franklin D., Stuart H. Starr, and Larry K. Wentz. *Cyberpower and National Security*. Washington, D.C.: National Defense University Press, 2009.

Krepinevich, Andrew F. "Cyber Warfare: A Nuclear Option," *Center for Strategic and Budgetary Assessments*, 2012.

Krepinevich, Andrew F. *7 Deadly Scenarios*. New York: Bantam Books Trade Paperback, 2010.

Liang, Qiao, and Xiangsui,Wang. *Unrestricted Warfare*. Beijing: PLA Literature and Arts House Arts, 1999.

Mao, Tse-Tung, and Samuel B. Griffith. *On Guerrilla Warfare*. Urbana: University of Illinois, 2000.

Moffat, James. *Complexity Theory and Network Centric Warfare*. Washington, DC: CCRP Publication Series, 2003.

Montross, Lynn. *War through the Ages*. New York: Harper, 1960.

Nye, Joseph S. *Soft Power: The Means to Success in World Politics*. New York: Public Affairs, 2004.

Paret, Peter, Gordon Alexander Craig, and Felix Gilbert. *Makers of Modern Strategy: From Machiavelli to the Nuclear Age*. Princeton, NJ: Princeton University Press, 1986.

Peikari, Cyrus, and Anton Chuvakin. *Security Warrior*. Beijing: O'Reilly & Associates, 2004.

Sun, Bin, Samuel B. Griffith, and Hart Basil Henry Liddell. *Sun Tzu the Art of War*. London: Oxford University Press, 1971.

Taleb, Nassim. *The Black Swan: The Impact of the Highly Improbable*. New York: Random House Trade Paperbacks, 2010.

Thomas, Timothy L. *Cyber Silhouettes, Shadows Over Information Operations*. Fort Leavenworth, KS: Foreign Military Studies Office, 2005.

Thomas, Timothy L. *Decoding the Virtual Dragon, Critical Evolutions in the Science and Philosophy of China's Information Operations and Military Strategy*. Fort Leavenworth, KS: Foreign Military Studies Office, 2007.

Thomas, Timothy L. *The Dragon's Quantum Leap, Transforming from a Mechanized to an Informatized Force*. Fort Leavenworth, KS: Foreign Military Studies Office, 2009.

Thucydides, Robert B. Strassler, and Richard Crawley. *The Landmark Thucydides: A Comprehensive Guide to the Peloponnesian War*. New York: Simon & Schuster, 1998.

U.S. Deputy Secretary of Defense. *Definition of the Term Complex Catastrophe*. Washington, DC: February 19, 2013.

U.S. Joint Chiefs of Staff. *Chairman's Strategic Direction to the Joint Force*. Washington, DC: Joint Chiefs of Staff, February 6, 2012.

U.S. Joint Chiefs of Staff. *Joint Operations*, Joint Publication 3.0. Washington, DC: Joint Chiefs of Staff, August 11, 2011.

U.S. President. *National Security Strategy*. Washington, DC: Government Printing Office, May 2010.

U.S. President. *Sustaining U.S. Global Leadership: Priorities for 21st Century Defense*. Washington, DC: Government Printing Office, January 2012.

U.S. Secretary of Defense. *Department of Defense Strategy for Operating in Cyberspace*. Washington, DC: Government Printing Office, July 2011.

U.S. Secretary of Defense. *Quadrennial Roles and Missions Review Report*. Washington, DC: Government Printing Office, January 2009.

U.S. Department of Homeland Security. "Critical Infrastructure Sectors." U.S. Department of Homeland Security. http://www.dhs.gov/critical-infrastructure-sectors (accessed February 25, 2013).

Wright, Quincy. *A Study of War*. Chicago: University of Chicago, 1983.

Verton, Dan. *Black Ice: The Invisible Threat of Cyber-terrorism*. New York: McGraw-Hill/Osborne, 2003.